CAERLEON

'Scenes Past'

A Walk Through History

by Norman Stevens

Dedicated to my Father
Ernest Stevens
1908-1997
A man of principle and integrity.
Who did leave this world a better place.

Foreword by
Councillor Jim Kirkwood, F.R.S.A.

Old Bakehouse Publications

Abertillery

First published in November 1997
Reprinted in March 1998

ISBN 1 874538 71 9

Published in the U.K. by
Old Bakehouse Publications
Church Street,
Abertillery, Gwent NP3 lEA
Telephone: 01495 212600 Fax: 01495 216222

Made and printed in the UK
by J.R. Davies (Printers) Ltd.

Foreword

by Councillor Jim Kirkwood, F.R.S.A.
Chairman Caerleon Urban District Council 1968
the last Chairman of Gwent County Council 1995/96

Photograph: Phil Bird, A.B.I.P.P., A.R.O.S., B.Ed.(Hons.)

For the past thirty-seven years I have had the honour and pleasure to play an active role in the education, social, sporting and public life of our town, Caerleon.

Therefore, I consider it a privilege to have been asked to write this foreword to Norman's 'Caerleon - Scenes Past', because he has portrayed what local people and our many visitors from all over the world, cherish about Caerleon.

In the early 1960s the Caerleon Urban District Council played an important and active role in housing part of the large influx of the personnel who were to work at the newly constructed Spencer Works Steel Plant at nearby Llanwern.

Since then Caerleon has grown tremendously both in size and population, as well as becoming a very attractive tourist centre, to be recognised by many as being the 'Jewel in the Crown' in the County Borough of Newport.

Norman's 'Journey on Foot' as he refers to it in his book, is a credit to his dedication and the intensive work undertaken in the production.

I know from personal experience, as a local Councillor, that Norman has an insatiable thirst for knowledge, a person whom I always welcome at public meetings, because he can be relied upon to make that meeting an enjoyable experience.

Along with many friends, neighbours and colleagues, I wish Norman every success in his efforts to ensure that OUR TOWN goes down in history as a warm and hospitable place to both live in and to visit.

Well done, Norman

Jim Kirkwood

Introduction

My interest in collecting postcards and photographic views of Caerleon started some thirty years ago. I have always had a feeling for the romance of the pictorial past and as my collection grew and having transferred these scenes to slides, the thought occurred that perhaps I should make them available to a wider audience. The most effective method of presenting them in a permanent way for all to enjoy, I perceived therefore would be through the pages of a book.

This book is not a history of Caerleon although it is historic in the views that have fortunately been captured on film. The photographs have been sequentially arranged to portray a journey through the town by foot, starting on the west side of the town bridge and following a logical route dictated by the locations of the pictures themselves. I have tried as far as practicable to give as much information regarding the content and location in order to create and sustain interest. It follows that many of the views will, at first sight, appear to be similar until closer examination of the detail is given. The passage of time and progress so created will show that change is all around us, barely noticeable until looking back when nostalgia or memory stimulates us to suddenly remember places, people or events of long ago.

To the many, who so generously loaned postcards or photographs and their willingness to share their private and often personal scenes, and have them recorded, hopefully for posterity, my most grateful thanks. As a social document of how things used to be, I hope that those who look at the following pages will derive as much pleasure from them as I did in assembling the collection.

Norman Stevens

Caerleon

The area on which Caerleon stands has been a site of habitation over many thousands of years. The Lodge Hill has been confirmed as an Iron Age fortress site, the presumed capital of 'Belin' one of the Kings of England in ancient times, with a large metropolitan city below. In AD74 the Roman Empire expanded its boundaries and came to occupy and settle in the area. In AD290 political changes in Rome led to the garrisons being withdrawn and the subsequent period has little recorded history. People were still here though using the Roman buildings and constructing their own designs, making use of Roman materials. During medieval times Caerleon began to flourish as a port and manufacturing region and for an extensive period, was the principal port along the coast during the late 19th century. With the gradual increase in size of vessels and the relatively shallow river at Caerleon, it had to be that the mouth of the river was where development could take place. Thus it was, the future of Newport and its deep water docks were to prosper at the expense of a declining Caerleon. Nevertheless the town has still remained a very desirable place in which to live. With the awakening interest and proper exploitation of all, its extremely varied history is gaining a worldwide reputation for its unique heritage in a superb setting.

Part One

The Journey begins, Newport Road to Caerleon Bridge
High Street to the Square
The Square
Backhall Street, The Priory to the Broadway
The Endowed School, Teachers and Pupils
The Museum and St. Cadoc's Church
Lodge Road and Roman Way
The Roman Amphitheatre
The College, Town Hall and St. Cadoc's Hospital
Goldcroft Common to Station Road
Station Road
The Railway and G.W.R. Station
Ponthir Road to Mill Street and Castle Street
Over the Bridge to New Road
Ultra Pontem
Journey's End - Look back from Belmont Hill and Catsash Path

Part Two

Civic Leaders, Organisations, Groups and Events

Street Plan of Caerleon

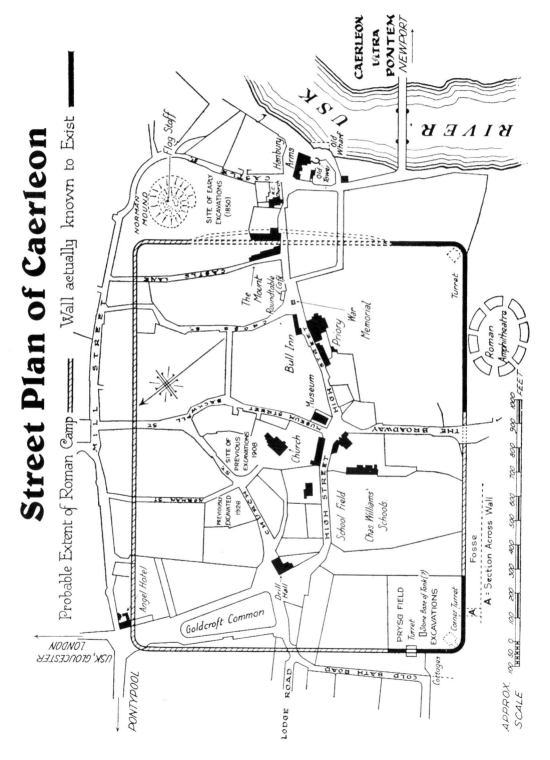

Probable Extent of Roman Camp ▨▨▨▨

Wall actually known to Exist ▬▬▬

Caerleon & Village.

ARMS OF KING BELIN FOUNDER OF CAERLEON
B.C. 410.

Caerleon Museum & Church.

The Coat of Arms above has apparently evolved through interpretation of legends and myths through the ages.
Below is the adaptation from the Arms of Hywel ap Iorwerth, Lord of Caerleon in the second half of the twelfth century.

From about 1924 is this tranquil scene of a sailing boat heading in the direction of Caerleon.

A view from the left bank and careful study will reveal the remains of the commercial wharf just this side of the bridge. The present owner of 'Bridge House', Mrs. Lewis informed the author that remnants of a tramroad track and turntable still exist beneath the driveway.

At a low tide some fishing boats can be seen drawn up on the river bank. The period is the early 1900s and local boat-building was carried out at Ultra Pontem at one time.

The view on this occasion shows a full tide with a number of boats on the river with salmon nets. This was quite a common sight when this picture was taken in 1910.

This picture gives an excellent view of the site of the wharf wall which originally extended up river to the Hanbury Inn. Before the development of Newport Docks, this was a very busy area handling both cargo and passengers. The wharf was quite likely refurbished when the bridge was built around 1805-1810.

A general view of Caerleon showing the flood plain fields with their distinctive drainage patterns, the land being suitable only for grass growing and animal grazing.

Above is a close-up photograph of the bridge taken in 1909. This stone-built bridge was completed in the year 1810 to replace the old wooden construction which crossed the river via Bridge Street at the eastern side of the Hanbury to Ultra Pontem. This original wooden crossing was permanently damaged by serious flooding in 1779. The view below is from a picture postcard produced some ten years later than the one above. On the reverse the sender writes of having a 'fine leave' at Caerleon, and as the year is 1919, they are probably the words of a serviceman having just returned from the First World War.

Five brave souls are seen rowing up the river in 1903. Newport Rowing Club regularly rowed to the Hanbury Wharf from 1900 to 1920 and used the inn for their meetings. During these early years of the twentieth century, Mr. John Sherwood an Oxford Blue, was landlord and brewer at the Hanbury. The rowers' clubhouse was on the banks of the River Usk at Shaftsbury Park. Just visible on the left of this picture is a white hoarding which was used for advertisements for the one-time Empire Theatre at Newport.

A prominent view of 'Wharf House' or Bridge House as it is now known, some 50 years after this photograph was taken. The wharf was used for commercial cargo until the building of a stone bridge at Newport prevented large ships from reaching the Caerleon moorings. Also, the opening of the Monmouthshire Canal took further trade away. Records show that the last cargo-carrying vessel sailed from Caerleon in 1896. She was a collier named the 'Black Prince' with a Captain Bennett in command.

The little girl seen here is in period dress pinafore in about 1903. Over the bridge can be seen 'Arnold Florist and Fruiterer' occupying the site since transformed into a garage. Mr. Arnold lived in adjacent Bridge House.

Looking towards Ultra Pontem with the Ship Inn at the end of the bridge. Near the river-bank is a 'living van', a contraption which would have been towed by steam rollers to house road-working crews, possibly working on the nearby new road. Just visible is some lattice ironwork on the bridge parapet, this evidently was once part of the old Newport Bridge.

What must have been a major accident for the era, is recorded in these two pictures. The date was October 6th 1919 when a speeding army vehicle from Caerleon went out of control and landed in the precarious position seen here.

The Hanbury Garage around 1926/1927 and a young Mr. R.R. Bennett is seated on his belt-driven BSA motorcycle outside his newly established business. In the background, wearing the flat hat is brother Ruben. The business was run by the same family from 1926 until 1963 when Gordon the son retired. Gordon incidently was named after the famous Brooklands motor racing driver and aviator.

April 1939 with 'Rusty' Bill Beech and 'Musty' Gordon Bennett the proprietor's son, both young apprentices. These were days prior to electrically driven fuel pumps, the Shell brand of petrol sold here being dispensed by the old fashioned hand pumps. Another artefact seen on the right is a tall early type cigarette machine.

Two later photographs of the Hanbury Garage from around 1946. Petrol was still strictly rationed after the war but at least modern electrical pumps have been installed. Parked outside in the upper picture is a Morris Commercial 5 cwt. van from the 1930s. Notice in the photograph below that the building is now adjacent to the roadway and field wall.

The years have advanced to 1953 for this photograph of a much modernised garage. The old building was demolished in 1949 with the accompanying bungalow being built in 1947. Gordon Bennett is seen standing back to the wall talking to the driver of an aged 1950s Austin Devon van. Note also the former traffic lights needed to regulate vehicles over a narrow bridge which in those days had a footpath on either side.

Some local advertisements and an old stoneware 1/2 pint beer bottle produced by John Sherwood of the Hanbury. This collectors piece was discovered in an earthbank at Llanhenock.

This is a copy of an old print showing the original wooden bridge and gives an excellent insight into the life of 18th century Caerleon. The bridge was connected to Ultra Pontem on the opposite bank and allowed coaches to travel to London on the coaching road which ran past the Bell Inn. In 1771 the bridge had reached a poor state of repair and was closed until new timbers had been inserted to strengthen it. Shortly after repair, on the night of October 29th 1779, heavy floods carried away the centre section together with a Mrs. Williams who happened to be crossing at the time. She had in fact been crossing the bridge to assist her husband home from his night out at the White Lion, Ultra Pontem. Mrs. Williams was swept aboard the timber downstream to Newport Bridge, when it struck the piers and immediately broken into bits. Fortunately she had the presence of mind to sit astride a larger piece and so continue onward, until at last her cries for help were heard by the master of a small vessel. The vessel managed to overtake the floating remnants of the bridge and rescue the terrified Mrs. Williams almost at the river mouth where it meets the Bristol Channel. It is recorded that she suffered no injury other than shock! The White Lion public house is still to be seen although now a private residence.

The Hanbury Arms as it looked in about 1920 with the old medieval tower on the left. The children are sitting in the middle of a disused Bridge Street.

The Hanbury Arms Inn, built in 1565 as a town house, named 'Ty Glyndwr', for the Morgan family, they later moving to Llantarnam Grange in 1593. The cobbled surface of the main road can be seen when the photograph was taken in the 1920s and still to be seen today in 1997. The bay window projecting towards the river is where Alfred Lord Tennyson sat when he stayed at the inn in September 1863, during which time he wrote 'Idylls of the King'. He wrote 'the Usk murmers by the window and I sit like King Arthur at Caerleon'. A plaque commemorates this in the room.

The stone tower is thought to be part of a fortified pair of towers. A similar one would have stood on the opposite bank, probably for protection of the port and bridge in medieval times, by having a chain stretching between to impede surprise visits by pirates or channel raiders. Caerleon had a Royal Charter granted by King Edward II in 1324, recognising it as an important port, trading being done across the English Channel with France and other continental countries. Also there was much domestic traffic to the Severn Estuary and Bristol Channel ports.

The inn was ultimately named after Richard Hanbury, the Ironmaster, and used his Coat of Arms as the sign around 1750. Prior to this the building was used as a private residence and trading took place from this house to a wide area across the Bristol Channel. The Riverside Room was used as a Magistrates Court in the 17th century with the round tower providing the lock up.

One of the local fishing boats under sail. Boats such as this often sailed the length of the Usk and into the River Severn. Fishing and boat-building in the area was a long-established means of earning a living in days gone by. The stone and flint building seen on the right is the pub brew house.

A view from 1929 shows that the brew house has been demolished and 'Nailery Cottage' has been built on the centre right. There is also a good view of the slipway with the river walls appearing in good order.

Two turn of the century pictures of old Caerleon. To be seen is St. David, Julius and Aaron Roman Catholic Church and priest's house. The buildings were erected in 1885 on ground given by local landowner Dr. Robert Woollet MD, JP, who lived at the 'Mynde'. Dr. Woollet also met the cost of the buildings, the house at the time being named 'Ty Craig'. On the right is the Hanbury with a walled courtyard with the earlier photograph above showing no need for a pavement. Below in about 1906 a pavement has been added although the roadway is still fairly rough.

A passive scene from 1912. The horse and cart belong to the Newport Steam Laundry owned by George Greenland and Sons, Bath Street Newport. Looking closely one can also see some other reminders of the past such as a wicker-work pram, a lady cyclist and a brave chicken crossing the highway.

Circa 1905 and a glance down Bridge Street (now High Street) towards the Hanbury Arms. The brew house on the left shows the pub brewery sign, the owners at the time being the Eastern Valleys Brewery Co. Ltd. The brewmaster and 'mine host' was a Mr. J. Sherwood. The advertising board promotes a performance at the Lyceum Theatre Newport by Mr. Frank Fenton and another sign proclaims 'Cyclist's and Boating House'. The young ladies are stood behind the pony and baker's trap of A.R. Williams Caerleon's baker who also had a grocery shop in the High Street.

On the left Mr. Berry's shop has a nice display of somewhat precarious potted plants (Caerleon in bloom 1911 style perhaps). Miss S.J. Richardson Family Butcher has a display of joints of meat with a patient dog waiting under the window. Miss Richardson's mother, with the same initials, is listed in a Directory of 1899 as having a butcher's shop in Cross Street. This might be considered unusual for a mother and daughter both to be involved in a business of this type.

The Square

A typical scene at the Square in 1903. The Bull Inn with its cobbled forecourt, some draught horses at rest, whilst their owner is probably inside and some young lads dressed in period Eton collars. The photograph below taken a year or two later shows a lone railway porter with his hand cart, probably delivering some luggage forwarded by visitors to the town.

The village postman and an inquisitive dog pose for the cameraman in about 1910. A popular postman at this time was Mr. Thomas Phillips who lived in Norman Street. The White Hart with its ornate frontage was at this time owned by a Mr. Tom Herbert, a local businessman who also ran a coal merchants and brickmaking concern. The shop next door is seen to have its windows protected by boarded shutters, possibly against unruly customers from the adjacent tavern?

Some features of this early scene include the delivery horse and cart waiting outside the butcher's shop of Miss S.J. Richardson. In those days there was a slaughterhouse and stockyard at the rear of the premises and cattle would often be seen driven from surrounding farms to meet their fate. Also note that the gas lamp standard on the left has lost its glass cover although Berry's shop nearby has some very ornate exterior lights.

Stood outside the Bull Inn is landlord Charles Talmage with his family. The house next door and stone building are now demolished and the site has become a car park. Two very old posters are to be seen on the wall of the pub, one advertising Miss Daisy Jerome probably appearing at the Empire Theatre Newport and the other promoting Lloyds and Yorath Stout from the brewery in Cambrian Road, Newport.

As always in the early 1900s, the Square was peaceful and safe from traffic. Just in the background can be seen the old grocer's shop of G.F. Thorne of Cross Street.

The years have moved on a little and the first signs of motorised transport have appeared in the Square.

Entering the Square in the early 1920s in their motor car are Mr. and Mrs. P. Berry proprietors of the drapery and stationer's shop as seen behind the car. The premises nowadays constitute a restaurant called 'Drapers', owned by a distant relative Mr. Stan Berry.

The corner butcher's shop was taken over by Mr. William Skuse in 1921 and he is seen here with his young son John and assistant Wilfred Waters. The young lad John was aged three when this photograph was taken in 1925 and he continued in the trade to become a master butcher with premises in Caerleon.

In the 1950s John Skuse, who had inherited the business is pictured outside the same shop with his gleaming vehicle for the period, an Austin A40 estate car.

Circa 1930 and the pub has changed its name to Ye Olde Bull, the owners at the time being Lloyds and Yorath of Newport. Parked outside and facing Cross Street is an old model T Ford complete with fabric covered body.

The year is about 1905 with a picture of W.J. Bennett of No.1 Cross Street advertising as an agent for 'Norman' cycles and motor works, for all your motoring needs with petrol sold by the can. These are the first premises in Cross Street, next to the Bull Inn and a fine array of early motorcycles is gathered. Two other traders' premises in the background are Bishops Refreshment Rooms and William Bishop's saddlery shop.

Still a quiet place to be, the Square in 1928. The War Memorial erected to honour the heroes of the 1914-1918 conflict consists of a water fountain and a fashionable new gas lamp to replace the old standard.

A 1930s look at Ye Olde Bull and parked outside just visible behind the War Memorial is a Trojan van belonging to Hunt Brothers of Blackwood. Hunts were leather manufacturers who regularly came to Caerleon to purchase animal skins from I. and W. Banner the local fellmongers. Tan House Drive is named after the nearby area where the business was conducted.

A Newport Corporation Tramways and Omnibus Co. single-deck bus leaves for Newport on Route Number 2, to the terminus in Skinner Street. There was a tragic accident in 1943 when a schoolteacher, Miss Rushbridge, who was evacuated with her pupils from Dover High School for Girls was killed whilst cycling to her home in Cross Street. She was knocked down by an Army truck travelling in convoy through the narrow High Street, an incident which led to the introduction of the one-way system in Caerleon.

Caerleon and District War Memorial which was dedicated on Sunday 29th May 1921 and unveiled by Lt. Colonel Evill, D.S.O., T.D. Officer Commanding 1st Monmouthshire Battalion. The memorial scheme was developed from the 'Welcome Home Fund', the organisers raising a mighty £1250 for the cause.

The monument is constructed of Cornish granite with bronze tablets listing details of the fallen. This photograph was taken shortly after the unveiling and the mother with her young boys probably had a poignant reason for studying the dedications on the wreaths. In 1966 the memorial was moved to what is now known as the 'Memorial Garden' next to the town hall.

A local hero who survived the Great War 1914-1918 was Sergeant W.T. Edwards D.C.M. William Edwards was born in 1888 at Ultra Pontem, leaving school at the age of 12 to work at Little Bulmoor Farm for two years before moving to work for the contractor building Newport bridge. He then joined the Army in January 1915, the 11th Battalion South Wales Borderers arriving in France in December 1915 as part of the 38th (Welsh) Division, later transferring to the Labour Corps in 1917.

William was severely wounded at Mametz Wood, Ypres in Belgium before eventual discharge in September 1919. For his gallantry during the conflict he was awarded the highly prestigious Distinguished Conduct Medal and the citation in the London Gazette of 13th February 1917 read as follows. 'For conspicuous gallantry and devotion to duty, he has repeatedly displayed great courage and determination on patrols, on one occasion rescuing a wounded officer'.

The war diary of the 11th Battalion indicates that this action took place on 15th May 1916 and the officer was a Second Lieutenant G. Moore. Sergeant William Edwards D.C.M. passed away in January 1958. His son, also named William now residing at Liswerry, donated his father's decorations to the S.W.B. Museum at Brecon where they are now displayed. The medals pictured below, are the D.C.M., 1914-1915 Star, British War Medal and Victory Medal.

To

H. J. Waters

who served in Britain's fighting forces during

The World War
September 1939, to August 1945.

We, the People of Caerleon

honour with Pride and Thanksgiving the Valour of our Sons and Daughters whose Steadfastness and Courage prevailed against Evil, and shielded us from subjugation.

"Thus shall we go more honourably."

The Second World War lasted for six years and above is seen a picture of Mr. Herbert Edward Waters one of many local inhabitants who fought for King and Country yet again. He served in the Royal Engineers Regiment completing his service as a Company Sergeant Major. After the war he took employment with the Urban District Council as Works Superintendent until retirement in 1967.
On the right is a copy of the certificate that was awarded to local inhabitants who fought and served during World War Two.

This section of the book concludes with a final look at the Square as it appeared in the early 1950s. A pre-war Ford 8 stands outside the closed 'Berrys shop' and on the railings behind the memorial an enamel sign indicates the way to the air raid shelter.

Backhall Street, The Priory to The Broadway

Backhall Street in the year 1910 with two prominent licensed premises of Caerleon, the Red Lion on the right and on the left, a little further on, with the large gas lamp, the White Horse.

An interesting 'Pub Token' which was unearthed by a member of the local metal detector club in a Caerleon field in 1986. This 3d (3 pence) brass token, about the size of today's two pence coin would have been in use in the middle of the 19th century. William Jones as inscribed on the token was proprietor of the Red Lion from 1858 to 1866.

The Priory which was built on land given by Hywel ap Iorweth, Lord of Caerleon, in about 1179, to the monks of 'Strata Florida' to build an Abbey. They found Caerleon to be too noisy for their liking and so moved to nearby Llantarnam and built there. Three monks and a priest remained at Caerleon to administer to the local population. The building here was owned by the Morgan family by the 16th century and altered to their taste using Roman materials from ruins in the area. It still has a church-like entrance with heavy oak door opening to an original flagstone passageway. The Photograph dating from about 1905 shows in the distance, on the left, the hanging signboard of the 'Three Salmons' pub which is now a private residence.

Pictured in around 1907, the Priory when it was the home of Colonel Sir Arthur Mackworth Bart and also of Humphrey Mackworth J.P. Here, the lawn is set for a game of croquet. Nowadays the building is a popular hotel, the entrance to which is through an enlarged doorway beneath the canopy seen on the left.

Looking up Broadway and on the right is the gate lodge and rear entrance to the Priory. The large Georgian house is Priory House, previously known as Broadtowers and on the left is the Endowed School. The tall chimneys in the background belong to the headmaster's house kitchen.

A closer view of the ivy-clad lodge and gates as they looked some 90 years ago. The photograph below dates from the 1930s and shows a fine view of the drive. The authentic thatched roof was unfortunately destroyed by fire during the 1980s and replaced with slates.

The 'Roman Arch' with the rear of the Priory in the background. The term 'Roman' is true only in that it was constructed from stone retrieved from local Roman remains. Built in about 1820, at the behest of a Miss Elizabeth Morgan who had taken up residence, it was considered most fashionable to have classical or Roman remains as features on one's property.

From days when hunting was an accepted sport in the area is this photograph of a meet of the Llangibby Hounds at the Priory in 1910.

Looking towards The Broadway, circa 1905 the Endowed School is seen on the right with 'Broadtowers' on the opposite side of the road. The object in the centre of the photograph is the remains of a gas lamp standard.

Caerleon Endowed School was constituted by the Charles Williams Foundation which was established in 1724. Williams was a wealthy benefactor who had made his fortune trading in eastern countries principally as a fig merchant in Turkey. The girls' dormitory was in the dormer roof space and boys' on the first floor. Teaching was confined to the classrooms on the ground floor, all originally lit by tallow candles changed to gas around 1875 and electric in the late 1920s. The school was originally founded for the education of thirty boys and twenty girls.

An exceptionally early photograph of the boys from the Endowed School, Class 2 in about 1890. At the back, far left is Mr. Evan Davies the headmaster who was in office from 1880 until 1923. Pupils at Caerleon originally wore uniforms similar to 'Blue Coat' School Westminster, London.

Another school photograph of the 1890s, this time the Infants Class III. Pictured far left is Miss S.E. Stott who was appointed headmistress of the Girls' School in 1892 and served until 1923.

Standard I Boys' department in 1928. Sat on the far right is student teacher Miss Wadley and a very young Jim Waggett is seen in the middle row, second from the right.

The Infants' Class of 1931 sat at their desks for the cameraman with Vera Waggett in the front right.

A fancy dress party organised for the Endowed schoolchildren in 1933. Two of the teachers are stood on the right, with Miss Thomas as the guardsman accompanied by Miss Toose.

An annual school party photograph from about 1934 with Head of the Girls' School, Miss Morgan sat in the centre.

Circa 1936 and the theme of the party dress appears to be worldwide national costume. Amongst the many familiar faces to be seen is that of teacher Miss Alice Shierson who is at the rear with a large white circular headdress.

An additional picture from the school during the 1930s and amid the pupils, in the centre is Miss Morgan.

This picture was taken in 1986 before the 1994 demolition of the kitchen extension to the left of the headmaster's house which was part of the school main building.

The Museum and St. Cadoc's Church

The Museum of Roman Antiques appearing as it did at the turn of the last century. The museum was originally built at a cost of £407 and opened to the public on 2nd August 1850. Some of the material used in this construction was retrieved from the old Market House which once stood on the Square and demolished in about 1847. Roman pillars also from the Market House were used to support the museum's ground floor. Timber from an old battleship of the George IV era, HMS Collingwood was put to use as roof supports after the ship was purchased as scrap from a Newport dockyard. In the closer view of the museum seen below, the signboard indicates an opening period of April to October with an admission charge of 3d for adults and 1d for children (less than $1^1/2$p and $^1/2$p respectively). School parties were admitted free!

In urgent need of repair and modernisation, the old building was demolished in 1986 except for the portico, which was salvaged and retained for the reconstructed premises. Below is a side view of the treasured portico carefully supported by scaffolding.

1988 and a completely reconstructed and refurbished museum replaces the 19th century building.

St. Cadoc's Church which stands in the centre of the plan of the Roman Fortress of Isca. The present church dates from Norman times although previous places of worship are believed to have stood on this site. It is largely constructed of stone from ancient Roman buildings although numerous alterations and modifications have taken place over the years. Of particular interest is the clock which was installed in 1887 to commemorate the Golden Jubilee of Queen Victoria. Pendulum operated, it was manufactured by W. Potts and Sons of Leeds and is wound up each week by the captain of the bell-ringers. It has a peal of eight bells making it one of only four in the country having a complete octave.

The lych gate of St. Cadoc's photographed in the 1920s. The gate was completed on 28th June 1919 and bears the inscription 'To the glory of God and those who fell in the Great War'.

The house seen on the left was once the home of the church beadle, a parish officer appointed by the local vestry to maintain order in church and local area. Over the years it had many uses including a storage for grain, a malt house, coffee shop, a fish and chip shop and art retailer selling Caerleon pottery. The building was pulled down in the 1960s and the site is now occupied by a bench seat for weary tourist travellers to rest.

A superb early view of the church with Museum Street to the right. Characteristic of this early 1900s scene is the gas lighting and also an early form of pushchair. Just noticeable on the right is a circular stone which was placed to protect the wall as horses and carts turned the corner.

St. Cadoc's church choir in 1959 and where possible the author has traced some names. Back row, left to right: Rev. Ivor Davies, Basil Reeve, Glyn Davies, Master Anstee, David Hovell, Jim Waggett, Paul Jones, Geoff Davies and Douglas Davies (assistant organist). Front row: Terry Swales, Godfrey Perkins, Geoff Waggett, Simon Fry, Phillip Hovell, unknown, unknown, Tony Fry, Dale Summers and Vernon Thorn (organist and choirmaster).

The choir a few years later in 1963. Rear left are Mr. Greener (Churchwarden) and Mr. Thorn with Mr. Tom Shierson (Churchwarden) far right. The following members of the choir went on to take Holy Orders. Top left: Rev. Donald Pope, Rector of Grosmont and Rural Dean of Abergavenny. Back row, second right: Rev. Stuart Dean, Vicar of Church of John the Baptist, Hadlam Parish. Middle row, extreme left: Rev. Geoffrey Waggett, Rector of St. Glynorrwg, Afon Valley, Bridgend. Chorister Jim Waggett, third row, Henry West Centre, Tim West (son) centre of boys.

The interior of the church in about 1933. The pointed arches are all that remain of the Tudor church.

Until 1948 Caerleon racecourse was the home of the Welsh Champion Hurdle Race, later to be renamed the Welsh Grand Annual Handicap Hurdle Race when it was transferred to Chepstow in 1949. Caerleon racecourse was registered for National Hunt Rules and well-equipped with a grandstand. It eventually closed in 1948 and was situated on land now occupied by the Comprehensive School and surrounding area. The 'Tredegar Challenge Cup', presented by Lord Tredegar to be raced for at Caerleon, having been won by Colonel Llewellyn riding 'State Control', was presented by him to Chepstow racecourse following closure of Caerleon. The hills of Catsash form the skyline.

Lodge Road in 1922 with the noticeably narrow bridge over the railway line. The previous wooden bridge was some 100 metres towards Newport and the scene of a railway fatality; whereby a fireman was knocked from his locomotive and killed, so low was the crossing. The G.W.R. were compelled to construct the new bridge seen here with improved clearance.

A view of the remains of the Roman barracks looking towards Lodge Road from the Fosse Way. On the skyline can be seen the then 'Monmouthshire Training College for Teachers'.

Two former scenes of public transport serving Caerleon. Above is Gwladys Place terminus for the Caerleon-Newport service in 1967 and below a more modern 1980s Metro Cammell Weyman one-man operated bus is pictured at Anthony Drive.

NEWPORT CORPORATION TRAMWAYS AND OMNIBUS SERVICES.

Service No. 2.

NEWPORT—CAERLEON.

Monday to Friday.

Buses start every half-hour from 7.30 a.m. to 12.0 mid-day, and every 20 minutes from 12.0 mid-day until 11.0 p.m.

NEWPORT (Skinner Street) :
First Bus departs 7.30 a.m.   Last Bus departs 11.0 p.m.

CAERLEON COMMON :
First Bus departs 7.30 a.m.   Last Bus departs 11.0 p.m.   (11.20 p.m. Clarence Place).

Saturdays.

Every 20 minutes from 8.0 a.m. to 12.0 mid-day, and every 10 minutes from 12.0 mid-day until 10.0 p.m., and every 15 minutes until 10.0 p.m.

NEWPORT (Skinner Street) :
First Bus departs 7.30 a.m.   Last Bus departs 11.0 p.m.

CAERLEON COMMON :
First Bus departs 7.30 a.m.   Last Bus departs 11.0 p.m.   (11.20 p.m. Clarence Place).

Monday to Saturday.

Early Morning Bus.

NEWPORT (Skinner Street) depart 5.45
CAERLEON COMMON   depart 6.10

Sundays.

Every hour from 9.30 a.m. to 2.0 p.m., and every 15 minutes from 2.0 p.m. until 10 p m.

NEWPORT (Skinner Street) :
First Bus departs 9.40 a.m.   Last Bus departs 10.0 p.m.

CAERLEON COMMON :
First Bus departs 10.0 a.m.   Last Bus departs 10.5 p.m.   (10.20 p.m. Clarence Place).

The amphitheatre with Christchurch in the distance and views of Ultra Pontem and Belmont House on Belmont Hill. This photograph shows the arena where gladiators pitted themselves in trials of strength.

The year is 1927 and there is a 'dig' in progress sponsored by the Daily Mail. The project was led by Dr. (later Sir) Mortimer Wheeler and some 30000 tons of soil were excavated. Sir Mortimer later achieved national fame as a television celebrity during the 1950s.

The 'Ermine Street Guard' re-enact scenes of 1500 years ago in the amphitheatre during the 1980s. The arena was capable of holding 6000 spectators equal to an entire garrison and was completed the same time as the Coliseum in Rome.

The Rt. Hon. Nicholas Edwards M.P. Secretary of State for Wales is seen here opening the Roman Baths at Caerleon in April 1985 and the guard of honour is provided by the Ermine Street Guard.

The College, Town Hall and St. Cadoc's Hospital

The Monmouthshire Training College, shortly after the opening in 1914 with some work still to be done to landscape the grounds. In 1996 it became 'The Caerleon College of the University of Wales'.

Laying the foundation stone of the Monmouthshire Training College, by the Rt. Hon. R. McKenna, M.P. Her Majesty's Home Secretary on Thursday 18th July 1912. A night of excitement preceded the event when some local supporters of the Suffragette movement set fire to materials on site. This was to show support for those of their members held in prison and on hunger strike, in order to obtain the right to parliamentary and council vote. The blaze was quickly discovered and extinguished.

Two photographs illustrating how impressive this building really is. The picture above was taken to show the completion of the driveway and below the college has been photographed to give a full view of its extent perched at the top of the hill in splendid isolation.

Caerleon Town Hall was originally used as a Drill Hall by the Volunteer Regiment of the 2nd Battalion Monmouthshire Regiment. It was built around 1780 by a Robert Fothergill Esq. one of the early tinplate works owners. By the early part of the 19th century however, the building had fallen into a very dilapidated condition, much to the dismay of the residents of Caerleon until the intervention of a couple of local men. It was felt that a place of entertainment would be most appreciated and Mr. Evan Davies, later to become headmaster of the Endowed School and Mr. Gilbert Harding, master of the Industrial School came to the rescue. Following the necessary renovation, the hall was given for public use in 1876.

The adjacent building was erected for use as the custodians' dwelling also housing a reading room and library. The agreement which conveyed the property for public use also stipulated that the land adjoining, should have 'no building erected upon it' and should be used as an 'ornamental plot for the enjoyment of all the people of Caerleon'. The War Memorial was re-located here from its original position in the Square in 1966. Records show that all of the buildings were taken over by the Caerleon Urban District Council in 1936. Today, the seal of the council can be seen in relief stone work on the top front pediment which depicts a 'Castle Triple-Towered'. This was adapted from the arms of Hywel ap Iowerth, Lord of Caerleon and an early Welsh prince during the second half of the twelfth century. The function of the buildings as council offices and chambers came to an end in 1974 with the reorganisation of local government and the Urban District Council being incorporated into the responsibilities of the Newport County Borough. The photograph above was taken in about 1906.

A view which would be difficult to repeat nowadays as the cameraman took this picture from the top of the boiler house chimney at St. Cadoc's Hospital shortly before demolition.

An aerial view of the hospital from about 1920. Construction of the hospital commenced in 1903 with the official opening taking place in 1906. Major re-routing of the land around the perimeter was required, with a new road built to make use of the new bridge over the railway called Lodge Road. The narrow white line crossing the field at the top of this photograph is now the route of Lodge Hill. The hospital church can be seen in the foreground, with the Lodge on the right and just two private dwellings on the main road.

The years have advanced to 1948 and it is useful to compare this photograph with the previous page to note some changes. Roman Way Estate has arrived together with some 'prefabs' and gradual house-building at Lodge Road. The extensive hospital grounds were very efficiently managed providing a constant source of fresh vegetables and flowers. Labour was mainly provided by the patients themselves, a theraputic facility sadly lost these days due to stricter imposition of health and safety acts under the new regional hospital board. In the 1960s the home farm was put up for sale and has since been used for house-building.

A view from the south side with the main railway line running north. St. Cadoc's was opened in 1906 by the Mayor of Newport, Councillor Frederick Phillips J.P. and cost £150,000 to build. It was so designed, that additional blocks could be added in future years with minimum disruption to the patients or staff. Initial accommodation was provided for 368 patients. The caption on this early postcard uses the archaic term lunatic asylum. Fortunately there is today, a much better understanding of the illnesses that can beset all levels of the population.

Caerleon Common and the roadway to the right was relatively new when this picture was taken around 1904.

A postcard from 1910 showing a few changes from the previous view. The tree has been pruned and the ivy is making progress over the front of some houses. The sender of this card has marked his house with an 'X' and at the time the occupiers were Captain and Mrs. C.S. Wilcox.

The Llangibby Hunt meet on the common outside the Drovers Inn. The photograph dates from around 1908 when a Mr. Edward Johnson was licensee at the inn. November was the usual time for the meet though in later years Boxing Day became the most favoured.

The Drovers and neighbouring houses have been recently decorated for this 1920s view. Previous spaces have been filled and the bay-fronted house is a recent addition. The single storey building with projecting porch is the Primitive Methodist church which was built as early as 1814. After 1933, by which time it had fallen into disrepair, it was used by a Mr. Baulch as a monumental sculpture works. In 1950 the building was demolished and the site used for construction of a private dwelling with a garage below.

A differing view of The Common showing on the right, The Croft with the front of the short row of houses with the Angel Hotel. The Croft, after many changes of use is now the basis of the Caerleon House Nursing Home.

Seen again some 90 years ago, is the Common with the prominent Croft on the right with a substantial brick wall to give it some privacy. At the time of this picture, the Croft was the home of Alderman Tom Parry J.P. later to become Mayor of Newport. Thomas Parry seen here on the left, was chiefly responsible for initiating the construction of the Talybont Reservoir. This was a massive project designed to supply water to and on behalf of the Newport County Borough Council to the town and surrounding area. Part of Caerleon's much loved common was presented to Councillor Parry in 1891 by the grateful citizens and was used for the building of the Croft. Another old establishment to be seen on the left of the photograph above is the Goldcroft Inn opposite the white painted building.

Goldcroft Common is the last survivor of nine commons of Caerleon and is now only a quarter of its original three acres.

A pleasing scene captured by Cardiff photographer Ernest Bush. The houses and pubs actually run with their foundations on the remains of the north wall of the Roman Fortress.

The late 1920s and seen approaching is the Newport bus, the service having commenced in 1926. On the left is a large advertising hoarding exhorting the wonder of using electricity, a novelty in Caerleon at the time! From 1845 a two-horse omnibus service operated from Newport to Abergavenny, passing through Caerleon and Usk and by 1875 the first dedicated Newport to Caerleon service was in operation both by private companies.

Two typical village scenes. Above, young children are only too pleased to pose for a photograph in about 1911, a period when the Methodist Chapel is beginning to show signs of disrepair with the rendering starting to fall away. The whitewashed house across the road from the Drovers is 'Allstone Cottage', built more than 300 years ago using stone from Roman ruins. Below, the gas standard is without its all important glass covering, possibly now disused and awaiting the arrival of modern-day electric street lighting.

The Goldcroft Inn as pictured in the 1960s. The front is pebble-dashed and changes are to be noted to doors and windows. The Goldcroft was originally a coaching inn dating from the 16th century complete with thatched roof and stables. The bar area of the pub still retains the original flagstones.

Early 1930s and two popular shops of the period are seen on the right. Tom Morgan was the butcher and Garfields the newsagent was next door. Other memories from the past include an old style telephone kiosk and motorcycle and sidecar.

A similar scene as previously pictured when some twenty years have passed and a more modern styled red telephone kiosk has been installed.

The Broadwalk before the First World War. In those days it acquired the cynical title of Salmon and Bloater Street due to the quality and size of its housing and perceived social standing of its occupants. The left side was Salmon and the right Bloater, possibly influenced by the differing widths of pavement?

Looking up Station Road towards Ponthir. To the left are Gibbens the Wheelwright's and a corner supply stores. Behind a patient horse with its trap, is the sloping roadway which led to the railway station.

Station Road

The corner of Station Road and the Common in 1900, with Gibbens's premises. John Gibbens came with his family from Taunton in 1886 and the family home, incorporating the works building, was built in 1890. He came as a journeyman wheelwright and at the outbreak of war in 1914, was building gun carriages for the military. Later on, due mainly to the shift working and noise created during unsociable hours, production was transferred to Twyn Oaks on the Usk Road. The business finally closed during the 1960s although the original building remains and has seen numerous changes and occupiers since.

A picture of John and Emma Gibbens and a typical bill for work submitted in 1927.

Looking up an almost deserted Station Road in about 1912/13. Above, the traffic consists of a horsedrawn milk cart on the corner and an early bicycle. The large house quite prominent in the background was once the home of Mr. William Buck, owner of the Pentwyn Coalmine at Pontypool. In the middle of the road a young boy collects some 'fertilizer' while two young girls await with the home-made cart. Below, another shop has opened in the row and the village policeman strides purposely up from the station. Also, it appears that a small boy is running over the bridge watched intently by the girl stood near the pavement.

Looking down Station Road which was formerly known as Railway Street. The houses on the left were built in 1900 and hold a little mystery. Soon after completion, the builder, a Mr. Morgan who lived in the nearest house seen here, departed from Caerleon leaving his property and contents behind and was never heard of again. Mr. Morgan was officially declared 'dead in law' in 1917. A young porter is seen on the right making his deliveries from the station just passing A. Jones the Grocer and Baker's shop.

The same end house as above in Station Road, on the corner of Railway Terrace (now Usk Vale Drive). This was the first orphanage in Caerleon and on the transom glass over the doorway is inscribed 'St. Cadoc's Home', although the home was in use only for a few years. Using land given by Viscount Tredegar, a purpose-built home was opened in Norman Street and paid for by public subscription. The foundation stone was laid by Lord Tredegar on 14th September 1907. The building was vacated as a home in the 1970s and is now used by the Autistic Society and named Orchard House.

A number of shops in Station Road decorated for the Coronation of King George VI and Queen Elizabeth in May 1937.

On the left is a scene from Station Road in 1934, the former Lloyds Bank and confectioner and tobacconist L. Coopey. The building was originally bought by Mr. Lewis Coopey's father to establish his son in business. Locals may also remember Marjorie Coopey working in the shop for many years who eventually married Lewis in 1935. The Coopey family terminated the business during the early 1960s and it is now a general store owned by Mr. V. Patel. Below is a later photograph from 1953 showing the bank having been converted into a shop for Marjorie Davies.

A Newport Corporation Tramways and Omnibus Co. Leyland Lion 32 seater bus stands in Station Road Caerleon. This particular coach was built in 1928 and remained in service until 1942. The motorised service which commenced in 1926 offered a return fare from Caerleon to Newport for 7d (3p) and the company was forced to reduce it to 6d (2^1/2p) to face competition by the G.W.R. who charged just 4d (1^1/2p) for the journey by train! At the time the buses had a distinctive livery of brown and cream.

Skinner Street in Newport which was the terminus for the No.2 Newport to Caerleon service. The year is 1934, two-way traffic is no problem and William Powell was on the screen at the Olympia.

Great Western Railway.

PERIOD HOLIDAY TICKETS

are issued EVERY FRIDAY and SATURDAY (until October 30th) from principal Stations in all parts of the country to NEWPORT (Mon.), situate 3 miles from CAERLEON, e.g. :—

London 23/9 (to Caerleon direct 24/-), Reading 17/9, Leamington 16/-, Warwick 15/9, Stratford-on-Avon 13/6, Birmingham 16/3, Swansea, 9/9, Liverpool 25/-, Manchester 26/6, etc., etc.

Available for return following Friday or any subsequent day up to and including following Sunday fortnight.

Frequent local train service between Newport and Caerleon.

CHEAP DAY AND HALF-DAY TICKETS ARE ISSUED TO CAERLEON OR NEWPORT from any districts, including Gloucester, Cheltenham, Hereford and Bristol, etc., also from CAERLEON and NEWPORT to many local places of interest, including GRAND CIR-CULAR TOUR OF THE BEAUTIFUL WYE VALLEY.

WEEK-END TICKETS are issued at about a single ordinary fare and a third from any station where fare is in operation. Forward Friday (after 4.0 a.m.) return following Saturday, Sunday, Monday or Tuesday. Forward Sunday return same day or following Monday or Tuesday.

Full details of services and suggested trips on application to Divisional Superintendent's Office, G.W.R. Newport ('phone Newport 4991 (extension 210 or 285).

DO NOT FORGET your copy of "HOLIDAY HAUNTS." Price 6d., obtainable at all Stations and Bookstalls.

G.W.R.—THE HOLIDAY LINE.

A 1930 advertisement

Circa 1905 and a two-coach local stopping train has just arrived. Noticeable on the coaches are stepping boards for use where certain platforms were below normal height. On the right of the bridge is a tall signal post, designed to give the engine drivers travelling towards Newport an early warning, as the curve of the line leading into Caerleon is the longest continuous curve in the country.

This picture was taken just after that on the previous page as the train has departed but the newspapers are still waiting to be picked up from the platform. The railway was first opened to goods traffic by the Pontypool, Caerleon and Newport Co. in September 1874. Passengers were being conveyed to Newport High Street the following December 21st. Although registered as a separate company, its headquarters were at Paddington and was really a front for the G.W.R. during the early days of a bitter battle to establish dominance between rival railway companies.

The up-platform embankment is decorated with whitewashed stones depicting Gt. Western Rly. Caerleon with the G.W.R. coat of arms and crown flanked by the date 1911. This was to celebrate the coronation of King George V. The signal is down, ready to allow the departure of the saddletank loco - with coaches lit by oil lamps, for Newport and there appears to be plenty of activity in the goods yard.

Around 1930 there is a busy platform, with guard and his flag at the ready and a very clean-looking side tank engine heads the train. At the time passengers could travel to Newport first class for 6p return and to be more economical a third class return was just 4p!

Two photographs from the 1950s with panier tank engines making steam. Above, the carriages are being propelled by the locomotive, with the driver in a special compartment in the leading coach. By this method the driver maintained control of the engine by connecting cables and vacuum brakes whilst the fireman remained in the engine cab. The photograph below shows the more popular method, engine in reverse and pulling the train to Newport.

The exact date is 20th June 1957 and the photograph has been taken from the bridge on Lodge Road looking in the direction of Newport. Just visible in the background through the smoke and steam is what looks like another bridge but actually are some service pipes from St. Cadoc's Hospital. Bottom left is the former signal box which was removed in 1962, amidst all the reorganisation of the country's railway system spearheaded by the eminent Dr. Beeching. Caerleon's Mr. John Barker served as signalman here for fifteen years and was the last in charge before closure. He recalls helping to install the modern electric multi aspect light signals and due to the urgency of the job, worked twelve hour shifts non stop for a fortnight. Work completed, he went on some leave on the Monday but on returning to work the following Monday, the signal box had vanished. His kit had been left for him at the station with instructions to report to Newport High Street. Mr. Barker also recalls an incident some years earlier, when he came on duty one morning to relieve the nightshift signalman only to find the signal box locked and the man slumped semi-conscious in a chair. He immediately forced an entry through a side window and noticed a strong smell of gas and consequently opened all the windows and revived his workmate. Many readers of this book may well remember gas being the source of lighting on our railway stations before electrification. Investigation of Caerleon's signal box problem revealed that salt had been stored beneath the building and consequently, over the years, had corroded the gas supply pipework.

When steam was King in June 1957 and an express passenger train, headed by engine No. 4997 Elton Hall travels north under Lodge Road bridge.

Again in June 1957 and a mixed freight train passes through Caerleon from the direction of Ponthir. In the background can be seen Penrhos Farm.

Signalling the 'beginning of the end' for the steam trains in April 1962. A 'warship' class diesel locomotive hauls a Manchester to Plymouth train through Caerleon non-stop.

All is quiet at the station on a summer Sunday afternoon in 1959.

Two additional photographs taken by Rev. R.W.A. Jones to remind the reader of the halcyon days of steam. Above, in about 1959 a 'Hall' class loco No. 7908 'Henshall Hall' heads an express towards Newport. Below, a 'County' class heads a fitted van freight train.

The station forecourt and approach road in 1962. The steps on the left, gave access to a footpath leading to Lodge Road and has a little story attached. The path was provided by the G.W.R. for the convenience of passengers, whilst a number of private houses had rear gardens backing on to it. Those occupiers whose gardens had gates therefore, were charged the grand sum of a shilling (5p) 'way leave' per annum for the use of the path. Just to further emphasise laws as they stood in days gone by, the path and road were closed once a year to deny forming a public right of way.

The distinct character of the nineteenth century stone-built bridge and station buildings at Caerleon are remembered here in 1962. For those who travelled this route it was always a pleasure to see an exceptionally well kept station. Even the stones on the embankment initialled BR for British Railways were kept whitewashed.

Above is a general view of the station and goods yard in 1962. Below and some twenty years later, there is little evidence left of the railway workings. All that remains is the main building and even that has been altered virtually beyond recognition.

1962 and Caerleon station is near closure. Looking up the line from Lodge Road bridge, the station yard is clearly in view. This area of course has now been redeveloped as a light industrial complex.

Stood for posterity on the 'up' platform are stationmaster Mr. Tom Forster with two of his staff, Mrs. Williams and a Dutch lady whose name can only be remembered as Tina. Locomotive No. 6946 'Heatherdew Hall' is seen hauling a Manchester to Plymouth express. Caerleon station was finally closed to passenger traffic on 30th April 1962 as the eastern valley services were withdrawn.

The Blades Works, Ponthir Road. The road runs behind the chimney stack with railway lines to the north in the foreground. Industry came here in 1756 with the opening of a tin plate works which used water power to operate a tilt beam hammer; although the site has seen many owners since. In 1946 William Hunt and Son 'The Brades Ltd.' bought the factory, producing agricultural and garden implements and tools. Time and changing economics forced the works to close in 1960, although during the ensuing years various trades and industries have brought new life to the area.

Cambria House as pictured in 1939 was built in 1858 as additional premises to the workhouse on the right. The object was to take in orphans and unwanted boys and train them for various types of work. Many children whose parents were in the Newport workhouse were also placed in Cambria but by 1902, with reforms to the system, all children were dispersed to 'homes'. The premises were purchased by Monmouthshire County Council in 1938 and then commandeered as an Army barracks and storehouse when war broke out in 1939. By 1956 the County Library was using the building for storage, eventual demolition taking place in 1982. The house on the left was the former residence of the master of the industrial school and workhouse.

Demolition has started on this fine old building in 1982 with the removal of the roof slates.

One hundred and twenty-five years of historic building lies in a pile of rubble as Cambria House meets its fate in 1982. The site was redeveloped and was the headquarters of the Gwent Ambulance Service until vacated in April 1997.

The Baptist Chapel which was built in 1764 held services in both English and Welsh until 1839 when changing congregations decided to discontinue the Welsh service on the 'Sabbath mornings'. The famous preacher Rev. Christmas Evans preached here in the 1880s and was known to attract huge congregations of six hundred and more! The long serving Rev. Dewi Bevan-Jones ministered to his flock here for forty years from 1866 to 1906. As is so unfortunately common now, attendances fell and the chapel eventually closed and was sold during the 1990s. The building has now been converted into two private residences, bodily remains exhumed and gravestones laid aside to form garden areas.

Over the bridge to New Road

A view taken from the bridge looking up the Usk in the 1930s with Ultra Pontem on the right bank.

Ultra Pontem in the year 1906 with some quite substantial fishing boats to be seen on the banks of the river.

Again, an exceptionally early view from the right of the bridge in about 1909 with Christchurch on the skyline, with Ashwell in the centre foreground.

Old Toll House, CAERLEON.

The Ship Hotel, New Road and the Toll House. The Toll House was built in 1825 after the new road in the centre of this picture was constructed. The road joined up with the coaching road at the bottom of Belmont Hill; an early by-pass for Ultra Pontem perhaps? A year or two later, in 1830, the Ship Hotel was built, obviously to catch passing trade on the new route. The photograph above was taken in 1904 when a Mr. A. Young was the licensee. It is interesting to note a number of private dwellings adjacent to the inn at this time, today these all form part of the Ship.

A lone pedestrian is seen in front of the Toll House in 1908. The house is interesting in that it has a blank window facing the road. This was a design ploy to avoid having to pay an early form of tax to the exchequer, the 'window tax'. To maintain symmetry the windows were so fashioned on alternate wall faces.

Circa 1947 and the Toll House is now seen in use as a private residence. Simmonds Brewery who were owners of the Ship Hotel at the time, is yet another familiar name to many, which has now disappeared amidst the world of takeovers and acquisitions.

Lulworth Road at Ultra Pontem in 1904. On the opposite bank can be seen the Hanbury Hotel complete with its Brew House.

Another charming view a little further down Lulworth Road. In those days it was probably safer to walk on the main road rather than on the roughshod pavements seen here! The picture dates from about 1910 and looks in the direction of The Hanbury.

A view looking towards the Bell Inn in about 1902.

Looking at the Bell Inn in about 1920 and this hostelry is believed to date back as far as the fifteenth century. By 1754 it is known to have been an important coaching inn on the road to Usk and on to London. It was a popular pick-up point and where the horses were changed and travellers refreshed.

Journey's End - Look back from Belmont Hill and Catsash Path

Two general views of old Caerleon, the upper photograph taken from the hill above the Bell Inn in about 1907. The lower picture from about 1938 shows Ultra Pontem, the old village across the river. The prominent white building in the foreground with vertical windows is the Church of the Holy Spirit. This was erected in the year 1814 as a non-conformist chapel for the Tabernacle Congregationalists, with pastors coming from Newport. In 1898 the building was taken over by the Anglican Church. It still remains a place of worship and is now known as the Mission Church. The church is situated on the old coaching road.

A turn-of-the-century photograph with Ashwell House in the foreground with New Road curving towards the bridge. The junction road opposite the house is the coach road to Usk.

Looking towards Caerleon from Christchurch Hill in 1919. In the distance can be seen the training college for teachers standing sentinel in solitary state.

A 'barrage' advocates dream, a full river! Looking into the far distance, it is possible to get some idea of the serpentine course of the River Usk, winding its way to the sea. It is also just possible to see the racecourse and grandstand between the trees. The racecourse at Caerleon saw great popularity until the interruption of the Second World War from which it never recovered, finally closing in 1948.

And so the journey has come to an end. We have been all around a most interesting and historical area that was once an Iron Age fortress, hamlet, Roman city, mediaeval village and now a prosperous small town, justly described as 'a very desirable area in which to live.'

The 1968 chairman of the Caerleon Urban District Council Mr. Jim Kirkwood with Mrs. Jean Kirkwood. Also seen in the photograph are some former council chairmen and chairman of the Caerleon branch of the Royal British Legion: T. Shierson (1959), Jim Waggett (1961, 1966), Col. E. Lyne (1955, 1965), Bill Lloyd (1960) and Eric Kilvington (1956).

One of the last civic ceremonies performed by members of Caerleon U.D.C. in 1974, tree planting on the small common opposite the Town Hall. Councillor Steve Veal the last chairman is seen here with the first spade of soil.

Council staff and their guests at a dinner held at the Priory Hotel in 1974 to mark the cessation of Caerleon U.D.C. Some of those pictured are Clerk of the Council Max Morrish, (centre standing) and the last chairman Councillor Steve Veal with his chain of office.

A Caerleon A.F.C. celebration dinner in 1966 with guest of honour Donald Anderson M.P. speech in hand. Also on the top table left to right are Tom Davies, Mr. and Mrs. Tom Whitfield, Mrs. Anderson and Chairman of the Council Mr. Jim Waggett.

A victory dinner held at Chepstow in 1966 to celebrate the achievements of Caerleon A.F.C. That year they were winners of the Welsh Amateur Cup, Monmouthshire Senior Cup and promoted to Division Two of the Welsh League. Among the many faces are Tom Whitfield (Manager), Monmouth Constituency M.P. Donald Anderson and Council Chairman Jim Waggett.

Caerleon as photographed from the air in 1932. Some landmarks to be seen include the old workhouse and industrial school on the right. Behind St. Cadoc's church is open ground with the telephone exchange building. The top of the photograph shows Lodge Road on the left with Station Road on the right. Bottom of the scene shows the Hanbury and the remains of former Bridge Street leading down to the crossing point of the previous wooden bridge to Ultra Pontem.

Two more aerial views which were taken in the 1980s. Above Home Farm is seen left of centre with Lodge Road running from lower right to upper left. Development of Trinity View has begun and Lodge Hill is in the upper right. The fields were once part of the hospital 'Home Farm'. The lower picture gives more detail of the hospital grounds with Home Farm Green, Home farm Close and Home Farm Crescent.

A superb aerial study from about 1989 where it can be noticed among other things, that new housing has started to encircle the ambulance depot.

Lodge Road at the start of the much needed road widening scheme in 1985.

Increased road traffic has caused many problems in many towns during the last two decades and Caerleon has not escaped. Lodge Road, scene of a number of accidents is seen here being re-developed with the Home Farm junction, Lodge Road and Trinity View. Below is a view of the work being carried out from a different angle.

John Skuse and his right-hand man John Griffiths display their expertise as master butchers by carving the ox roast at the celebrations held on Goldcroft Common in 1974 to mark 1900 years of Caerleon.

John Perry and colleague supervise the ox roast at the 1974 celebrations. The ox was provided by Mr. Ben George, owner and mine host of the Hanbury together with the Nolan brothers, earth moving contractors and Dr. Russell Rhys chairman of the festival committee. Roasting commenced at 6.30 in the morning and the beast was ready for carving at 7.30 that evening. All monies raised together with an Arts Council Grant were used to finance the Town Hall mosaic.

Commissioner Marjorie Phillips is pictured inducting Carole Stevens as 'Snowy Owl' with the 2nd Caerleon Brownie pack. On the left is 'Brown Owl' Billie Williams pack leader, the date being 15th December 1980.

A proud photograph taken at the Civic Centre Newport on 25th June 1986, the group having received the 'Flame of Friendship' from the Chief Commissioner for Wales.

February 1981 and Catherine Stevens graduates from the Brownies to the Girl Guides with Captain Joyce Roberts presiding.

Caerleon Girl Guides and Brownies attend the Newport and District Thanksgiving and Dedication Service Parade at St. Paul's Church Newport in 1986.

The Girl Guide Movement celebrated its 75th anniversary in 1985. Here are some of Caerleon's Guides and Brownies marking the event on Goldcroft Common.

Enthusiastic players of the ancient game of bowls at the opening of the Bowls Club in 1964. Godfrey Rowlands is about to bowl the first wood.

A photograph taken at the Caerleon Annual Fete on 28th August 1978. The smiling young ladies represent the Brownies' float depicting the winning team with the world trophy 'World Cup' winners, Argentina.

The Brownies with their flags representing the 1st, 2nd, 3rd and 4th Caerleon Brownie packs prepare for a church parade in July 1978.

Some local dignitaries are in attendance for an event at the amphitheatre in 1952, possibly the annual armistice service. Seen left to right are C. Evelyn Gough, William Povell, Godfrey Rowlands, Jack Duthie, Ernie Jordan and Jack Williams.

Inside the Town Hall in 1952 is this group of council officials. Seated are Russell Green (Clerk and Registrar), Ernie Jordan and Jack Duthie. Amongst those standing are William Povell, Benjamin Barker, Godfrey Rowlands, Eric Kilvington, William Lloyd, Mrs. Griffiths Jones, C. Eveleyn Gough, Col. C.E. Lyne and Jack Williams.

In keeping with national tradition on the occasion of a Royal Wedding, street parties are a must. This is the scene of Home Farm, Hazel Walk party, held on 29th July 1981 celebrating the wedding of Prince Charles and Lady Diana Spencer.

Caerleon Carnival 1979 and this particular entry by the Brownies is 'Aunt Sally and Wurzel Gummidge's Wedding and Guests'.

Continuing with 'Royal occasions', this is the party at St. Cadoc's Close to celebrate the
Investiture of the Prince of Wales in 1969.

St. Cadoc's Church of England Childrens' Home which was originally opened in 1908.

Pictured here are the young people of St. Cadoc's Childrens' Home who have just been entertained by Mr. Jim Kirkwood. The children were enthralled by the talk given of his travels to the U.S.A., Australia and the Far East to study steelmaking techniques through a scholarship of the Churchill Trust in 1969.

'Aunty' Kay Cheeseman and 'Uncle' Jim Cheeseman who were house mother and father at St. Cadoc's Home from 1960 until 1974.

Officers and N.C.O.s attend the presentation of some bicycles to the Childrens' Home in 1963. The 1st Queen's Dragoon Guards Regiment adopted the home and made regular visits there.

The remains of a 1948 Jowett Bradford van, once used locally by ironmongers Bergum and Davies, High Street (now Gareth Jenkins). The vehicle was given to Caerleon Comprehensive School as a restoration project, undertaken by the design, craft and technology department. Started in April 1979, the work was completed in June 1980. Many local companies gave materials and expertise towards the project such as Saunders Valves, Monmouthshire Timber Supplies, Coated Metals Ltd., Kingsway Service Station and Sufflex Ltd. Many generous donations were also received by school staff and helpers.

A complete strip-down of the aged van ready for chassis and mechanical rebuild. The custom-made body capable of carrying six passengers was eventually achieved after many hours of voluntary effort by staff and pupils.

The finished product, registered number LKJ 726 looking in pristine condition. Seen here are members of the Design, Craft and Technology Department who guided the project and helped raise funds. Left to right are David Prosser, Hywell Buckland (Head of Department), Neil Ingham, Thurston Lovatt and Jeanette Farr.

June 1980 and seen here are some of the boys principally involved in the work who gave a great deal of their own time, Ian Lawrenson, Christopher Worthy, Paul Webb, Mark Cullinane, Stephen Parsons and Michael Rothwell.

1982 and demolition of a once so familiar landmark at Caerleon, the chimney stack of St. Cadoc's is about to disappear for good. These are two views of the service road leading to the boilerhouse.

Acknowledgements

It is with sincere thanks that I readily give credit to those who generously allowed the loan of photographs and gave of their own time and knowledge.

Photographs: - Mrs. Marjorie Bennett, Mr. Nigel Bown, Mrs. Barbara Bees (nee Thomas), Mr. Jeff Bishop, Mr. H.G. Buckland, Peter Blagojevic, Mr. Phil Bird, A.B.I.P.P., A.R.P.S., B.Ed. (Hons.), Mrs. Angela Collingbourne, Mrs. M. Coopey, Mr. A.G. Davies (Caerleon Comprehensive School), Mr. William Edwards (Liswerry), Mr. Tony Friend, Mr. Bryan Ford, Mr. Ken Graham, Miss M. Gibbens, Mr. John Hodge (Haywards Heath), Mr. Phil Harris, Mr. David Hall, Mr. N. Ingham, Reverend R.W.A. Jones, M.Sc., F.R.Sc. (Newport Pembs.), Councillor J. Kirkwood, F.R.S.A, Mr. Mike Macleur (Newport Free Press), Mr. D. Prosser, Miss Molly Pitt, Mr. Ken Rees, Mrs. R.A. Richards, Mrs. Brenda Raines (South Wales Argus), Mr. Godfrey Rowlands, Mr. John Skuse, Mr. Doug Slatter (Newport), Mr. D.B. Thomas (Rogerstone), Mrs. Dorothy Taylor, Mr. Jim Waggett, Mrs. Dianna Waggett (nee Owen), Mrs. Billie Williams.

Time and Information: - Mr. Gino Alonzi, Mr. John Barker, Mrs. Lola Bennett, 'Copywrite' Newport, Caerleon Branch, Library Staff, Mrs. Melvina Dobbs, Mr. M.J. Everett, S.W.B. Archivist, Brecon, Miss Primrose Hockey, M.B.E., J.P. (deceased), Mr. Ken Jayne (Cwmbran), Margaret Jones (Caerleon), Mr. Thurston Lovett, Monmouthshire Railway Society, Newport Borough Reference Library staff, Mr. & Mrs. Vinodroy Patel, Dr. Russell Rhys, M.D., Mrs. Caroline Richards, Mrs. Hilda Thomas, Mr. Wilfred Wilson, Mr. Henry West.

My thanks also to Malcolm Thomas and staff at Old Bakehouse Publications for nurturing a beginner and to Councillor Jim Kirkwood for his Foreword.

It is my belief that more postcards and photographs of the past are still in existence, waiting to be recorded for the interest of future generations of Caerleon inhabitants. Please, look in your albums or shoeboxes! Even some showing signs of age and wear, all are acceptable. Many thanks.

Bibliography

'Trains and Buses of Newport' 1845-1981, *D.B. Thomas & E.A. Thomas* - Starling Press
'Guide to Caerleon-on-Usk', *W.A. Morris, Lt. Col. R.A.M.C., Retired* - Published 1931
'Newport Transport' 80 Years of Service, *E.A. Thomas* - Published by Newport Borough Council
'The Living Village', *S.G. Deane* - Village Publishing Cwmbran
'The History of the Monmouthshire Railway & Canal', *Aubrey Byles* - Village Publishing Cwmbran
'Caerleon Endowed School' 1724-1983, *Tim Morgan* - Starling Press 1983
'Caerleon Past & Present', *Primrose Hockey, M.B.E.*
'R.H. Johns' Newport Directories 1899, 1908
Great Western Railway, Ticket Examiners 1928 Fares Book
'Illustrated Guide to the Parish Church of Caerleon, *Stanley Knight & Ivor G. Mathews*
'Caerleon Heritage Trail', *Pamphlet produced jointly by Caerleon Civic Society, Local History Society & G.C.C.*
'Historic Caerleon' A Walk Around, *Pamphlet by Caerleon Civic Society, Researched by P. Hockey*
'Caerleon - Isca' *Roman Legionary Museum Booklet* - Published 1987, National Museum of Wales
'A Popular Guide to Caerleon' *by Isca and Atwood Thorne, M.B. (London)*, Published 1928 Western Mail
'Caerleon Endowed School' The First 270 Years, *T.M. Morgan* - Published 1994, Williams Schools Caerleon
'South Wales Argus' various dates
'Souvenir Programme Sat. 13th June 1987 to celebrate the opening of the Legionary Museum'
'Local Government in Newport' 1835-1935, *by John Warner F.L.A.* - Published Newport Corporation
'Hanbury Ale House', *Information pamphlet* - 1996
'Tavern Tokens in Wales', *Neil B. Todd* - Published National Museum of Wales 1980
'Historic Caerleon', *Official Guide of the Urban District Council* - 1955
'Caerleon: Isca', *with a sketch book, Harry Le Caux*
'50 Years of Racing at Chepstow', *by Pat Lucas* - Published H.G. Walters 1976
'Children in Exile', *Peter Hayward* - Published Buckland Publications 1997
'Caerleon Land of Legends & Legions'. *Pamphlet by Cadw* - 1997

Further books in this series are available from Bookshops or through The Publishers.

Blaenavon Through The Years in Photographs	**- Volume 1**
by Malcolm Thomas and John Lewis	ISBN 0 9512181 0 7
Blaenavon Through The Years in Photographs	**- Volume 2**
by Malcolm Thomas and John Lewis	ISBN 0 9512181 3 1
Blaenavon Through The Years in Photographs	**- Volume 3**
by Malcolm Thomas and John Lewis	ISBN 1 874538 10 7
Blackwood Yesterday in Photographs	**- Book 1**
by Ewart Smith	ISBN 0 9512181 6 6
Blackwood Yesterday in Photographs	**- Book 2**
by Ewart Smith	ISBN 1 874538 65 4
Brynmawr, Beaufort and Blaina in Photographs	**- Volume 1**
by Malcolm Thomas	ISBN 1 874538 15 8
Brynmawr, Beaufort and Blaina in Photographs	**- Volume 2**
by Malcolm Thomas	ISBN 1 874538 26 3
Remember Abergavenny	**- Volume 1**
by Louis Bannon	ISBN 1 874538 75 1
Collieries of the Sirhowy Valley	
by Rayner Rosser	ISBN 1 874538 01 8
The Flavour of Islwyn Remembered	
by Kay Jenkins	ISBN 1 874538 06 9
Bargoed & Gilfach in Photographs	**- Volume 1**
by Paul James	ISBN 1 874538 31 X
History of Webbs Brewery - Aberbeeg	
by Ray Morris	ISBN 1 874538 46 8
The District of Sennybridge, Trecastle and Defynnog	
by Gareth Jones	ISBN 1 874538 51 4